Gui

Your Step-By-Step Guide To Raising Guinea Pigs

HowExpert Press

Copyright www.HowExpert.com

For More Tips, Visit

www.HowExpert.com

Recommended Resources

<u>www.HowExpert.com</u>

- Short "How To" Guides by Real Life Everyday Experts!

Table of Contents

Recommended Resources 2

Introduction 7

What is a guinea pig and where does he come from?
    7

Why should I choose a guinea pig as a pet?   8

Why the animal is called a guinea pig?   9

Chapter One: Description of the Guinea Pig   10

Are there different kinds of guinea pigs? 10

Guinea pig breeds   14

Long haired pigs   14

Short haired breeds 14

What color is a guinea pig? 16

Chapter Two: Choosing a Guinea Pig   17

Guidelines for choosing a guinea pig: 19

Chapter Three: Setting Up Your Guinea Pig   21

What set up does a guinea pig need?   21

How do I choose a cage for my guinea pig (s)?   22

What do I put into the cage?   23

What should I feed my guinea pig?   25

Chapter Four: Green Food for Your Guinea Pig 28

Food for any guinea pig   29

How often do I feed my guinea pig?   30

Chapter Five: Socialization with Your Guinea Pig
          31

What do my guinea pig's sounds mean ? 32

What daily care does a guinea pig need? 33

How do I trim my guinea pig's nails?   33

How often do I bathe my guinea pig?   34

What daily care does his cage need?   35

Do guinea pigs need exercise?   38

Resting/sleeping   39

Handling/socializing with people 39

Socializing with other guinea pigs 40

Do guinea pigs play with toys?   40

Breeding and newborn guinea pigs   41

How do you sex a guinea pig?   42

How long does a guinea pig live?   43

Diseases in guinea pigs: 44

How do I know if my guinea pig is sick? 45

Can I take my guinea pig to a dog and cat
veterinarian? 45

Chapter Seven: Guinea Pigs and Other Animals
     48

Do guinea pigs get along with other animals?   48

Chapter Eight: About using guinea pigs for research
and guinea pig shows   51

Where can I meet other guinea pig owners?   51

Are there competitions for guinea pig owners? 52

What is judged at a guinea pig show?   52

Epilogue   54

About the Expert   55

Recommended Resources 56

Introduction

What is a guinea pig and where does he come from?

The guinea pig as we know the animal today is a small rodent and comes from South America, although some say he was brought to South America originally from Asia. His Latin name is cavia porcellus with a subspecies name of cavia cutleri. The name cavia is a name for any member of the rodent family, and the guinea pig is considered a rodent. The second part of his name, porcellus, is the Latin word for pig. In many parts of the world he still goes by an abbreviation of his first name, the cavy. He is genetically related to ferrets and chinchillas. He is found in the wild in Peru, close to the Andes mountains. In parts of southern and central America, he is bred and kept as a food source. He is supposed to be related to an animal that carries a similar-sounding name, the capybara. The capybara is a much larger animal, but is also an herbivore, or a non-meat eater, and is also found in the wild in South America, however, the capybara lives in and around water.

The guinea pig has been used as a food source and by "healers" throughout South America for many years to identify and cure diseases in people. An adult guinea pig is "rubbed" against the sick part of a person, then cut open to inspect its entrails, and based on what the "healer" sees in the guinea pig's insides, the sick person is treated accordingly.

Also, the guinea pig has been used in religious ceremonies, in particular solid black guinea pigs were and are popular for sacrifice.

Why should I choose a guinea pig as a pet?

The guinea pig is a small tail-less rodent, larger than a gerbil or hamster, weighing about 1 ½ to 2 lbs. He is a daytime animal and sleeps at night in contrast to hamsters, gerbils and rats, which are nocturnal and like to sleep during the day. This can explain why hamsters, gerbils and even rats can bite: they do not like having their rhythm disturbed and can bite when picked up during the day. The guinea pig is a clean animal, gentle by nature, is reasonably intelligent and has a life span of five to seven years. He is easy to care for and bonds easily with people.

He is the perfect first pet for a young child and makes a good pet for a kindergarten class. A guinea pig pet comes with lessons, too: he will teach a child about responsibility, compassion and nurturing. In return he will give lots of affection.

- The guinea pig is large and sturdy enough for young children to hold
- He is easy to care for
- He is easily socialized
- He bonds quickly to his humans and shows affection
- He is a daytime animal, sleeps at night

- He is clean, gentle and reasonably intelligent

Why the animal is called a guinea pig?

There are several theories as to where the animal's name came from. The Latin name for him is cavia porcellus, porcellus meaning "little pig." Why he was called a pig again could have several explanations: He could look like a small pig with a proportionally large head, stout body and round tail end. He provided meat for the natives and the sounds he makes could sound like a pig. He has been a food stable in South and Central America for centuries but was believed to have come there from French Guiana. So he would be a "Guiana pig," over time becoming a guinea pig.

Another theory is that when the Spanish explorers took the animal back to Europe with them, he became a popular pet in wealthy Europe, so that even royalty had pet guinea pigs, including the British royals. The explorers sold him for a guinea apiece, which was English currency at the time..a pig for a guinea = a guinea pig.

Chapter One: Description of the Guinea Pig

Are there different kinds of guinea pigs?

The guinea pig is classified by his coat. The Peruvian guinea pig is considered to be the oldest of the guinea pig breeds, and has the longest coat. While he is beautiful, he requires daily cleaning and brushing with a medium to soft brush or a short-toothed metal "slicker." He will also need a haircut every four-six weeks. He originates in the Peruvian mountains where it can be quite cold, and as protection from cold weather he has a long coat. His coat can grow to about 4-6" in length, divided in the middle by a "part" down the back of his spine. He will also have hair falling over his face, and with a heavy undercoat, it can sometimes be difficult to distinguish back and front of these animals. They are prone to carrying shavings, food and stools around in their long coat, and will require more care than the short haired pigs. A good solution -unless you are showing your pig in a guinea pig show- is to trim the coat around the rear end so it is short, that will help to keep the area clean. Also the hair in his face should be trimmed so he can see where he is going.

The Abyssinian guinea pig -the Abby- has a coat with "cowlicks" or whirls, in the guinea pig world called "rosettes." These whirls are symmetrically placed all over the body, about 8-10 in all. The coat itself is usually not more than an inch long, and with his whirls, he has a just-gotten-out-of-bed look. He will also have a band of raised hair over and around the nose, the so-called mustache. These pigs seem to be a little more skin sensitive, but enjoy a brushing with a soft brush such as a soft children's hairbrush or toothbrush. There should be two rosettes on the shoulders, one on each side, four along the back, two on each side, one on each hip and one on each side of the rump area.

The "silky," "smoothie" or "sheltie" guinea pig is another longer-haired guinea pig. He is different from the Peruvian in that his hair does not part down the middle of his back, it grows straight back from the neck to cover the entire body. He will not have long hair in the face or rear end, and his undercoat will not be as dense as the Peruvian. The texture of their coat is also different, the hair feels fine, silky and smooth, giving the breed its name.

Yet another longer-haired breed is the texel. He has a longer coat like the silky, but his coat is thick and curly, like a Brillo-pad. He has curls all over the body, including on the belly, legs and feet. He will sometimes have a part down his back. This breed, along with the Peruvian and the Silky, will require daily grooming to keep their coats in good condition. A guinea pig with a coat that is not groomed regularly can develop "mats" and these mats can cause severe skin irritation and be painful for the animal.

The short haired guinea pigs are probably the most common. There are various coats and coat combinations of the short coated pigs, including the American short haired pig, the Rex pig, the Teddy, the coronet and the crested pig. The short-haired pigs are also old breeds and are probably the first to be

domesticated. Their coats are shorter, about 1/2-1"
long, and are soft and lie close to the body. They
should be brushed daily with a soft brush. A good
investment for grooming these pigs is a baby's
hairbrush.

The Rex guinea pig has a short, fuzzy coat that
looks and feels somewhat bristle-like to the touch.
Even the whiskers are short, stubby and curly. These
pigs can be a little larger than the average guinea pig,
and the nails on their feet are thick and grow very
quickly, especially on the hind feet.

In contrast, the Teddy guinea pig's coat, while
also thick and fuzzy, seems to be a little softer, and
their whiskers are straight. This breed seems to be
bred a little smaller than the average guinea pig, and
requires time every day for brushing to avoid mats
and to avoid dragging shavings, hay, stools, etc.
around in their coats.

The crested and coronet guinea pigs are
relatively new breeds and are hugely popular. The
crested pig is a short-haired pig with a single rosette
in the forehead and the coronet pig is long haired with
a rosette. In most cases the body of the animal will be
of a solid color and the rosette in the forehead of a
different color, most often white.

A more recent breed is the hairless guinea pig.
While all other guinea pig breeds are born fully
furred, these hairless pigs are born hairless and do not
grow hair, except for wispy growth on the face, feet
and legs. Their bodies have wrinkles. These are not
animals for the beginner, they are extremely skin

sensitive and require warm temperatures and very careful exposure to the sun.

The body confirmation of the guinea pig is pretty similar for all breeds. They are short, chubby with a round rump and are tail-less. However, the longer-haired breeds tend to have a longer head and face with something of a "Roman" nose while the short-coated breeds seem to have a round face. The short haired breeds can be rounder in the body and measure pretty much the same all the way around from the shoulders to the hips. These are sturdy animals and make good pets for smaller children.

There are variants and combinations of these coats; you can for instance have a half Peruvian with wispy long hair a few places on the body combined with an Abyssinian, so that the rest of the body has a shorter coat with rosettes, and this makes the Abyruvian. Or you can have a short haired pig with a series of whirls along the spine, giving him a "mohawk"-like appearance. However, all the breeds except the hairless guinea pig can have a "satin" component, where the coat takes on a glossy, soft appearance. This is because each hair follicle is hollow.

Guinea pig breeds

Long haired pigs

The Peruvian guinea pig has a 4-6" long coat with a "part" down the middle of his back. He requires daily brushing to avoid matting, and unless he is to be a show animal, a good idea is to trim the face and the rear end.

The Abyssinian guinea pig has whirls, "cowlicks" or "rosettes" over his entire body, symmetrically placed. The coat itself is about 2-3" long.

The "silky", "smoothie" or "sheltie" guinea pig has long hair, about 4-6" long, but it grows back from the face and neck and covers the body only   and he does not have a part down his back.

The texel guinea pig has a curly long coat all over, including on the belly, and can have a part. They also have curly hair behind the ears

Short haired breeds

The American shorthair is the most common guinea pig. The coat is about 1" long and smooth, lies close to the body.

The Rex has short, fuzzy hair with stubby, thick curly whiskers. The nails on his feet are thick and seem to grow faster than the nails on other breeds.

The Teddy guinea pig has a coat like a child's teddy bear. His coat is short and fuzzy, but is soft to the touch and his whiskers are straight.

The crested and coronet pigs are short haired, solid colored pigs with a rosette of a different color, most often white, in the forehead, the coronet pig having the longer coat.

The longer haired guinea pigs have a curved, long head, sometimes called a "Roman" head, where the short haired breeds have heads that are round, although you can sometimes see rounder heads with the long haired breeds also. The American short hair can be chubby-looking, and is generally the sturdiest breed and the perfect first pet for a young child. He will not require long grooming/brushing sessions, although he will enjoy the attention. The long haired breeds will require daily brushing and grooming and even though they groom themselves, they do require help. A small "slicker" or steel-toothed brush is good for the curlier breeds, a soft children's brush is good for the silky-coated breeds. It is good to remember that the skin of a guinea pig is sensitive and that hard, forceful grooming is painful for them. I recommend that in the case of matting of the long, curly-haired breeds to apply a small amount of hand lotion/baby oil to the mats and then carefully untangle the mat without pulling on the skin. If that is not possible, the best thing is to cut off the mat.

What color is a guinea pig?

Guinea pigs come in a variety of colors and color combinations ranging from solid black and solid brown (called chestnut) to cream and white. There are two-colored and three-colored pigs in various combinations, as well as a "merle" color. The merle guinea pig has hair where the hair tips are a different color from the root of the hair, often white. The gray/white merle is sometimes called an "agouti." There are different colored brindle (striped) pigs, most often brown/red and black. There are Dalmation pigs with spots of different sizes and a beautiful tri-colored pig where the colors should be black, white and chestnut.

The tri-colored pigs are popular because of their symmetrical markings with white face, head and neck, chestnut brown upper body and front legs, then black in the lower body and hind legs, or they can have a brown or black face, a brown or black rear end and a symmetrical white stripe in the middle. These are sometimes called Dutch guinea pigs. There is also a cream colored pig that usually has dark eyes and is very striking. You can get a variation of this and have a guinea pig that looks like a Siamese cat with cream color on the body and dark ears, nose, eyes and feet. These are very popular pigs. Most pigs will have white on their feet, at least one foot will have some white. An all white pig is usually an albino guinea pig. He is totally white with very light or red eyes. The iris of the eye is clear, and the red showing through is really blood vessels behind the eye. These pigs are very light sensitive and require careful outdoor exposure to sun.

Chapter Two: Choosing a Guinea Pig

How to choose a guinea pig:

Choosing a pet takes careful planning. What kind of pet? What does he need? What does he eat? Where will he live? Male or female? Once you have decided to get a guinea pig and bring him home, you need to do some homework and decide where his cage should be. The guinea pig's cage should be about 2 x 3 feet per animal and placed in a spot where there is no direct sun, no drafts or cold air in the winter and no chemical fumes or smoke. Also, it should be in a relatively quiet spot, for while guinea pigs enjoy watching the comings and goings of people in a household, they should not be exposed to loud sounds or bright lights for long periods of time.

Once all has been decided and you've decided to bring home a guinea pig and you've decided on a young one, head to a reputable breeder/pet store. Look for a pup (also called a piglet) that seems to be curious and outgoing, not too skittish. He should be about three to four weeks old. He should be used to people handling him and not be afraid of being touched or picked up. Look at his eyes and nose: they should be clear and mucus free, and the eyes should be looking straight at you. The nose should be part of his curiosity and be twitching to get a whiff of you. Guinea pigs do not have the best eyesight, but their sense of smell and in particular hearing are very well developed. Look at his nails, they should be short and not curled under the foot. Listen to his breathing. If he is wheezing, sneezing or coughing, he has been exposed to cold and perhaps has a respiratory infection. Look at and touch his coat, it should be soft and smooth. Pay attention to bald spots on his body. He should have a small bald area behind each ear. Look at his ears for evidence of ear mites/ear infection. Lift his lips (guinea pigs have a split upper lip like a camel) and look at his teeth: Are they in alignment?

The uppers -guinea pigs have two very large upper teeth and two large lower teeth- and lowers should be over one another with the upper jaw closing over the lower jaw. He will, because of the large upper teeth, have an overbite. Jaw misalignment can make it difficult for the animal to eat properly, so he will perhaps be drooling and/or bleeding a little from the mouth. Look at the condition of the cage he is in: is it clean and is there enough space for him and his litter mates? Can you see stools/urine spots? Stools should be firm and brownish-green.

If you can pick him up, pay attention to his body weight: Does he feel compact, sturdy and tight or does he feel like a

Raggedy Ann doll and flop back and forth? Can you feel his spine or ribs? Does he screech when you touch him/pick him up? A continuously screeching guinea pig can have the beginning of a skin infection, and he will be in pain when you touch him; his skin will be tender to the touch. Turn him over and look for bald spots, signs of scratching on the belly. This might be a good time to sex your pig. If it is an older female, has she been kept with males? Is there a chance of pregnancy? A male guinea pig -a boar- will be a little larger than a female of the same age. If everything looks good and you decide on a forever home for the guinea pig, then you will need to invest in a home and its furnishings for the animal.

You can also make the choice to have two pigs, so that your pig is not alone if you are away from home during the day. Since guinea pigs are very social animals, they are happiest with a mate of the same sex. In contrast to other animals, even though the two guinea pigs will bond strongly with each other, they will happily include you in their social circle and quickly learn to accept you. With more than one animal though, perhaps it gives peace of mind to know that when you are away during the day your animal is not alone.

Animal shelters throughout the country have healthy and adoptable guinea pigs of all kinds, including the young ones. Often, because of lack of space, a shelter will put two pigs of the same sex together, and it would be very easy to adopt such a pair that are used to one another.

Guidelines for choosing a guinea pig:

- Watch him move about the cage and look at how he interacts with other pups
- Look at the condition of his enclosure, look for stools/urine and note the consistency of   the stools
- Pay attention to eyes, nose, ears and nails

- Examine, sniff and touch his coat
- Look at his teeth and jaws
- Lift him up and look at his belly, sex him/her.
- Ask about his age; is there a chance of pregnancy in a female?

Chapter Three: Setting Up Your Guinea Pig

What set up does a guinea pig need?

Once you have decided on where to put the animal's cage, you'll need to invest in a good and sturdy cage with metal grid sides. A 20 gallon aquarium can be a good solution for a female with very young pups, but an aquarium quickly gets too hot and oftentimes does not offer much room as the animals grow. A cage with a large door or opening on the top is good, makes it easier to clean the cage. A cage should measure at least about 24" x 36" per animal with metal siding (bars).

The cage should be kept in an area where there are no chemical fumes, tobacco smoke, excessive heat or cold. In other words, the cage should not be close to a window in the summer and should be protected from drafts in the winter. He should be brought indoors when the temperature goes below 60 degrees if he is an outdoor pig. While the guinea pig is naturally curious and enjoys watching the comings and goings of a household, he should not be exposed to loud, sudden noises, shrill doorbells or bright lights for longer periods of time.

In pet stores you can find a large cage with wire grid on all four sides and the bottom with a "drawer" or pan underneath that you can take out and empty. I do not recommend this kind of cage unless you put enough shavings in the drawer or pan to cover the grid on the bottom of the cage. Wire grid is painful for guinea pig feet, and the bottom of their feet can become bruised and sore. A toenail can get caught in the grid and the guinea pig can lose a toenail/toe. However, a metal cage with no wire grid on the bottom and a totally removable bottom drawer is a good option; this makes cleaning easy. Also if and when you take your animal outside, you can set the cage right down on grass and remove the bottom, thereby giving your pig access to fresh green grass while letting him keep his surroundings. He will enjoy this: It's his familiar cage with his food and water dishes. A word of warning, though: No pesticides or weed killers on the grass; these are very toxic to the animal. I do not recommend any wood on the guinea pig cage, guinea pigs chew and nibble on everything and can chew wooden framework to splinters.

How do I choose a cage for my guinea pig (s)?

- Look for a metal cage with sturdy sides, allow 2 x 3' per animal
- Look for a cage that has a large top or front opening
- Chose a cage with a "drawer" on the bottom that can be removed.
- Chose a relatively quiet area for the cage, away from heat, cold, fumes, sudden noises.

What do I put into the cage?

Starting from the bottom:

First: A good solution is to line the cage bottom with four to five pages of newspaper, which is easy to gather up and throw out -and it's good recycling sense. A wire cage with a wire grid bottom is painful for any animal to stand on, so if you have a cage with wire flooring, put a layer of 4-5 pages of newspaper over it. This will provide protection for the feet and will also be a catch-all for wet/soiled shavings and hay.

Second: A small layer of wooden shavings on top of the newspaper is good to absorb wetness, but do NOT invest in pine shavings or shavings with any kind of smell or coloring. (i.e. cedar). These shavings have been treated chemically and can be toxic to guinea pigs. Cat litter is not a good solution either; cat litter is too dusty for guinea pigs, and the small pebbles are hard on a guinea pig's feet. Sawdust is not good for guinea pigs either, it is too dusty. A good alternative to wooden shavings is the commercial corn-cob bedding made from recycled corn cobs. This is edible for pigs -they love corn and are constantly nibbling- plus it is relatively inexpensive. Both wooden shavings and corn cob bedding can be bought in most pet stores and in some supermarkets.

Another cage floor cover recycling idea (instead of shavings): Shred newspaper into long shreds and put about a 2" deep layer of paper shreds on top of the newspaper floor covering.

The next layer up is a handful of good, fresh alfalfa hay or an orchard/timothy-grass mix. This is sold commercially in pet stores/supermarkets. Look for the date on the bag, as the fresher it is, the better. Hay can develop mold in a closed plastic bag. If there is a feed store for large animals in your neighborhood, a "flake" of alfalfa or timothy-grass mix hay is very inexpensive and will last a long time. A "flake" is an increment of measure for bales of hay -used for larger animals: horses, cows, etc. - and equals about 1/10th of a bale of hay. If you are able to get a "flake" at a feed store (usually under $3.00), store the flake in a trash bag, but do not close the top; hay needs to breathe. A guinea pig will use the hay to graze on during the day and to hide and burrow in and under. However, do not give too much alfalfa, it is rich and can bring about runny stools. (Guinea pig stools should be dry. The stools should be checked daily.)

Another thing the pig needs is food and water and food and water dishes: A good sturdy food dish for his pellets is best. A heavy stoneware dish with straight sides is best, but not so big that he can get into the dish. Guinea pigs have bouts of serious activity during the day and in all the running around the cage, including what is called "popcorning," when he'll get shavings into the food dish. ("Popcorning" is when a guinea pig runs in circles, squeals and then jumps on all fours up in the air, turns around in the air and lands on all four in the other direction. This is happy behavior.) I recommend a hanging food dish, one that hangs on the side of the cage with screws, something like food/water containers for birds. These can be found at pet stores and will sometimes be included in the purchase of a cage.

Speaking of a water dish, a bottom water dish can be overturned and/or filled with shavings or feces and is a mess to clean. So a water bottle with a flusherball in it is the best way to go. This water bottle is sold at pet stores and in some supermarkets. The water bottle should be at least as long as the pig himself and cleaned every day. (Easy to do with a handful of small pebbles or marbles that you shake around in the bottle with a little water (no soap). The pebbles will get algae off the inside sides of the bottle. Rinse the small pebbles, put them in a container and use them again the following day.) Fill the water bottle with clean water and put the top on.

What should I feed my guinea pig?

The mainstay of your guinea pig's diet should be guinea pig pellets. They are sold commercially at pet stores and supermarkets, and at some pet stores can be bought in bulk. A piece of advice: Find the date on the pellet bag and go for the freshest one. Some plastic bags with guinea pig pellets sit on grocery store shelves for so long that the pellets turn moldy, and that moldy dust can be toxic to guinea pigs. The pellets are small, rice-shaped and dark green. The bag should clearly state that these pellets are for guinea pigs, which means that they are vitamin C fortified. The reason for this is that guinea pigs cannot by themselves produce/metabolize vitamin C and need to have vitamin C added to their diet daily. Pellets from a good animal food company will do that, and supplemented with leafy greens, the pig will have adequate vitamin C. The guinea pig should always have pellets available.

If you are close to a feed store and can buy your hay there in "flakes," the feed store may also have dried corn which has been broken into pieces, called "cracked" corn. This is used for chicken and bird feed, but guinea pigs enjoy cracked corn mixed in with their pellets and it is good for their coat. They also seem to enjoy "rolled" oats, which is a form of dried oatmeal oats. If you buy about a pound of each and add about a tablespoon of each to your dish of pellets every day, your pig's diet will be even better balanced.

With food and water containers, shavings, hay and newspaper, all you need is a small space for him to hide during the day where he can feel safe. Guinea pigs in the wild have predators both on the ground and swooping down from the air, so they will look for a place to hide. They do not dig holes or burrows themselves, but will temporarily take cover in someone else's burrow. An "igloo" from a pet store is a good solution, but a small box with a hole in the side works just as well, a small shoebox with a hole in the one end is good. Or an empty oatmeal canister where the both ends have been removed. Or a piece of PVC pipe that is a little bigger than his diameter. A prized "house" is a large elbow or T-joint of PVC, big enough for him to go into and perhaps even turn around. You can find these joints/pipes at any home improvement store, in the plumbing department. But anything that can be cleaned and that will give him a feeling of safety will do. Another good idea is a large, clean flower pot laid on its side. Remember, guinea pigs are prey animals and will look to hide wherever they can when they feel insecure/threatened or even just for a place to rest.

To recap, you'll need:

- A sturdy metal cage with a metal grid and a large door opening/ top opening.
- Newspapers to line the cage bottom.
- Shavings, non-cedar, not chemically treated, or corn cob bedding or shredded newspaper.
- Hay, orchard, timothy-grass mix or alfalfa.
- A sturdy food dish, stoneware, with straight sides.
- A hanging water bottle with a flusherball.
- Vitamin C fortified pellets (perhaps with "cracked" corn and "rolled" oats).
- A "house" where he can feel safe.

Chapter Four: Green Food for Your Guinea Pig

What greens do you feed a guinea pig?

Your guinea pig should have a handful of fresh greens every day. You can feed him either in the morning or in the evening or even stagger his greens throughout the day. He should have the greens as a supplement to his pellets. The guinea pig is happy with routine and repetition and learns quickly when to expect his greens. Guinea pigs love anything green: romaine lettuce and red leaf lettuce (not iceberg lettuce, which is mostly water and has very little nutritional content), apple (with skin), spinach, carrots and carrot tops, parsley, (especially good, it's full of their vitamin C), kale, collard greens, cucumber (with skin) , broccoli, arugula. If you have access to a pesticide free yard, dandelions and clover, especially the flowers, are wonderful treats.

Some guinea pigs are fruit eaters, some are not. Some enjoy a small piece of strawberry, a slice of banana, a little melon. However, watermelon seems to be a great favorite of almost every pig, both vegetable eaters and fruit eaters; they enjoy the wet sweetness and will often eat even the rind. Some pigs do not care for fruit but are instead vegetable eaters: green pepper, broccoli, cabbage, green beans, collard greens, even a small piece of sweet potato. I recommend trying just a tiny bit of strawberry one day and a bit of green bean or cucumber another day, and then watching what he picks up to eat. The teeth of a guinea pig -like rabbits' teeth- are constantly growing and they will need something hard to chew on every day to provide grinding of the teeth; such as an inch of raw carrot or a piece of broccoli stalk, so even fruit eaters will need a small piece of carrot/broccoli stalk.

Again, not more than a handful of greens every day so they can get their vitamins fresh daily but the mainstay of the diet is still the pellets. Another favorite vegetable of almost all guinea pigs is raw (uncooked) corn on the cob. However, corn is rich and can cause serious diarrhea/dehydration, so for a small pig (a pup) about 1/2" of cob/day is plenty, an adult pig can have 1 1/2". Simply slice the corn in small slices and put it into the cage; let the pig do the corn removal himself.

Food for any guinea pig

- Hay, alfalfa, orchard or a timothy-grass mix, two handfuls given fresh daily.
- Vitamin C enriched guinea pig pellets, refreshed daily.
- Fresh greens, either fruit (apple with skin, strawberry, watermelon) or vegetables. (romaine lettuce, arugula, spinach, carrots with top, parsley, green pepper, broccoli, cabbage and uncooked corn on the cob) -a handful given every day.
- Garden dandelions and/or clover dandelion

greens/flowers, or clover/clover flowers, pesticide free.

How often do I feed my guinea pig?

Guinea pigs are by nature grazers and move in large herds in the wild. A guinea pig should always have access to clean water and guinea pig pellets. It is generally enough to give him a handful of fresh greens once a day. But as the main part of his diet should be the pellets, he should have free access to pellets at all times.

Chapter Five: Socialization with Your Guinea Pig

What sounds do guinea pigs make?

Guinea pigs communicate using several different sounds: the happy whistle he gives when he sees you, the squeal/squeak when food is coming, a rumbling sound accompanied by side-to-side movements, teeth chattering, whistling and a soft almost purring sound. The squeak/squeal means he's happy, he knows food is coming and can't wait. Your pig will quickly learn to recognize the sound of the fridge door opening, the rustling of a plastic bag, and will squeal/squeak in anticipation. In sheer impatience he can also bite at the cage bars. The rumbling sound with the side-to-side movements is a warning sound.

He'll also chatter/gnash his teeth and raise the hair on the top of his neck and back in an effort to scare away other pigs, especially other males. The soft "purr" is a contented sound, happens with grooming, with snuggling and indicates your pig is happy and feels safe. There is also a low "rumble" sound or a "wheek" sound when something startles your guinea pig, for instance a telephone ringing, a doorbell, the ring of a kitchen timer, the jangle of a set of keys. This "wheek" is a distress sound and is often accompanied by "freezing," where he stands still and tries to figure out where the danger is and whether he should run away or not.

An item of trivia: The squeal/squeak sound that guinea pigs make has also given the animal a name. In South America, the guinea pig is known as the "cui" or "cuy," which could sound like the sound he makes.

What do my guinea pig's sounds mean?

- Squeak/squeal (in anticipation of something good happening)
- Whistling (a happy sound, like when he sees you coming in the door)
- Low rumbling sound accompanied by side- to-side movement and rising of the hair on the back of his neck and spine as well as teeth chattering or gnashing. This is a threatening sound and meant to intimidate other pigs, especially other males.
- "Purring," soft sounds indicating the pig feels safe and content.
- A "rumble" that is a startle sound (the sound of keys on a keychain, the doorbell, the kitchen timer.)
- A "wheek" sound. This is a scared sound and is usually made when the animal is frightened. He will stand in one place for several seconds, trying to assess what he thinks is danger. He will "wheek" to signal distress to other pigs.

What daily care does a guinea pig need?

As part of daily care and socializing, the guinea pig should picked up and handled every day. His coat should be brushed with a soft brush and if there are mats, these should be un-tangled. Feel his body all over, is he gaining weight properly, does he have cuts/bumps/scratches that are new and were not there previously? Look for mucus from eyes/nose, look for mites/mange on the skin, look into the ears and check for dirt, check his feet for long nails and check the soles of the feet for cuts or abscesses. (This can happen when the animal steps on a piece of hay, which then punctures the skin on the pad of the foot and creates an abscess.) The nails will have to be trimmed every 2-4 weeks or as needed. Guinea pig nails do not follow a regular time plan: some nails will grow faster than others on the same foot and will need to be trimmed even though the other nails on the same foot do not need trimming.

Gently lift his lips and look at his teeth. Are they OK? Does he have a cracked or perhaps broken tooth? Look at his face. If there is a small amount of milky-looking discharge from the eye, this is normal and is used to keep the eye moist. But if the animal develops crusty eyelids or an eyelid is swollen, the pig needs to see a veterinarian as quickly as possible.

How do I trim my guinea pig's nails?

To trim the nails: pick the guinea pig up and gently take hold of one of his feet. This is most easily done if his back is placed against your body for support, and the left hand takes hold of the foot to clip. White nails will have a dark center. This center is called the "quick" and is actually venous blood supply to the nail. The white or clear part of the nail is like our fingernails and needs to be trimmed back till it is at the same length as the quick in the center. Again, the hind legs have very long toes, three toes on each foot. The front feet have short, clubby toes and there are four on each foot.

There are small animal clippers available at pet stores, such as cat clippers or small bird clippers that can be used. If you should happen to nick the quick, apply pressure to the nail for a few minutes, and the bleeding should stop. There are products available to stop blood loss when the quick is nicked. These are called styptic powders and come in small jars. A good quick thing to do if you have nicked the quick is to press the animal's entire foot into the jar of styptic powder for a few seconds and the bleeding should stop. Again, a guinea pig's feet have their own time tables: one nail on one foot can have a growth spurt where the other nails are short. It is important to pay daily attention to the feet, but as a rule, nail trimming should be done about every 2-4 weeks.

How often do I bathe my guinea pig?

Guinea pigs do not like water and cannot swim. If your animal becomes dirty, usually all that is needed is for the dirt to dry and then be brushed out. If this is not enough, a moist, non-soapy washcloth to the dirty area is enough. Never immerse the pig into water, this will terrify him. If he becomes wet with the washcloth washing, do not use a blow dryer on him; the hot air is too hot, and the sound will scare him. It is best to towel dry him and then let him air dry.

What daily care does his cage need?

Look in his cage: wet shavings should be taken out of the cage daily and he should be provided with fresh and clean, dry shavings. And all the wilted vegetables should be removed;

he is either getting too much and cannot finish his vegetables/fruit pieces or his appetite is down. This is a good time for paying attention to his stools: more or less than the day before? Runny? Pick up the wet newspaper with wet shavings and soiled hay. After the wet newspaper with shavings has been thrown away, put 5-6 clean newspaper pages down again with clean, fresh shavings/corn cob bedding/shredded newspaper on top.

He should have a few handfuls of hay every day, the wet/soiled hay removed. His water bottle should be cleaned. The pellet dish should be cleaned and fresh pellets added. Pay attention to the water level in his water bottle: Is he drinking more or less? Once a day he should have his fresh greens, and to keep things interesting for the guinea pig, the greens can go in different spots every day so he'll have to "hunt" for the greens.

As a gnaw-toy, a piece of wooden tree bark is good, a small piece of natural wood used in bird cages is good as these they have been treated, cleaned and ground down for birds. Guinea pig teeth are continuously growing, and the animal needs hard objects to grind his teeth with; an inch of carrot, a piece of sweet potato and broccoli stalks are all good as well.

Some guinea pigs "play" with their water bottle and manage to dribble all over. They spend lots of time licking on the water bottle spout and seem to like the bubbles, the sound of the waterball and the water drooling all over their face. This is boredom behavior and should be stopped.

Pick up his "house" every day, wipe it off and empty it for stools, wet shavings and hay. Some pet stores sell small "tree houses"of hard wood shaped like a half barrel. These come in different sizes, and guinea pigs enjoy hiding under them. But because they are made of wood, a guinea pig can chew on the edge, so it will need to be checked daily for splinters.

An easy way to clean the cage in just a few minutes, especially if there is more than one animal, is to take the animal(s) out of the cage altogether, put them temporarily somewhere safe, (the kitchen sink is good -or in the bathtub), gather the wet newspaper layer with wet shavings and wet hay and throw it all away. Then put down clean, dry newspaper, clean shavings or corncob bedding and a handful of clean hay. Wipe off the "house," clean the water bottle, fill it, empty the pellets out of the pellet dish, clean it, add more pellets and put the animal(s) back into the cage.

Then put the filled water bottle in, put the clean pellet dish in and perhaps a sprig of parsley or two. This is a routine that takes just a few minutes and the guinea pig will quickly learn that when he sees you gathering newspaper, fresh hay and shavings, he can anticipate being picked up and taken out of his cage. He will also quickly know to then expect clean shavings, hay and perhaps a small treat. Most animals enjoy routine and repetition, and if your pig knows the time of day you clean his cage and can see you gathering newspapers, hay, etc., he will very quickly learn it's time to be picked up.

As mentioned earlier, it is imperative that guinea pigs be given a diet rich in vitamin C. Sometimes guinea pigs will pass stools that are bright green in color and appear to be more mucousy than normal stools. The pigs will eat these stools. This is normal as those stools contain essential minerals and vitamins. This is called coprophagia and is normal behavior for a guinea pig, both males and females.

When you put your pig back into a cage that has been cleaned, he may scoot his rear around the bottom of the cage. This is him marking his territory. He does this because the old, soiled shavings smelled like him and were home to him, but now the new shavings/newspaper is in and it doesn't smell like him, so he has to hurry up and put his mark on it. This is normal behavior in both males and females. Guinea pigs do not see very well, but their sense of smell and hearing is really well developed.

Do guinea pigs need exercise?

Guinea pigs do need exercise. In nature they roam in great herds and spend their days grazing on the ground, constantly moving. They are prey animals and constantly on guard for predators from the air (raptor birds), and from land carnivores. If they perceive danger, they will sometimes "freeze" for a few seconds, give a "wheek" sound and then scatter, burrowing into crevices and cracks in the ground. They do not dig or burrow themselves, but will borrow in some other animal's crevice. They are constantly on the move and cover large areas in a day.

If it is possible, a treat for an indoor guinea pig is a ground enclosure outdoors where he can feed on grass (no pesticides), dandelions and clover. Even if he is only outdoors for an hour or two every day, he can easily manage to eat a square foot or two of grass. He should never be left alone when he is outdoors, and he should not be exposed to direct sunlight. He should still have access to water and shelter.

If he is taken out of his cage indoors, a good option is to have a small children's wading pool with a little food and shavings on the bottom. A couple of small clean bricks in the middle of the empty wading pool will give him a chance to climb, which guinea pigs enjoy. They will climb to the highest point and look out. Some people put their pigs into an outdoor wading pool with a screen covering while cleaning the cage. The advantage of having a small wading pool is that it can quickly be emptied, rinsed out and stored until next time it is used. Some people will put their animals and a small treat in the kitchen sink while they clean the cage, or in the bathtub. Sinks and bathtubs should be cleaned thoroughly afterwards.

Whatever you choose, don't leave him outdoors without supervision. If he is indoors, don't let him run loose on the floor. He can come across electrical wiring, and chewing on that wiring can kill him. He can also hide under and behind furniture and will be difficult to corner/catch.

Resting/sleeping

Guinea pigs get tired and rest. They do not lie down and close their eyes like dogs or cats, but will put their heads down and briefly close their eyes. Because they are prey animals in the wild, they seem to sleep with one eye open and on alert. They rarely sleep for very long with both eyes closed. They will nap for periods of 15-20 minutes at a time both during the day and night.

Handling/socializing with people

Most guinea pigs enjoy being handled. They will sometimes even stand up in their cage, looking to be picked up. With time and a lot of positive reinforcement, you might get your pig to come when called. Once you hold them, they will sometimes lick your arm, hand, face, fingers. Some people say the licking is to get salt from our skin, I prefer to think it's simply giving kisses.   To pick up a guinea pig, use two hands, one around the chest and upper body and the other hand to support the rear end. And then hold him close to your chest. He will very quickly learn to settle down. A guinea pig urinates every 15-20 minutes, so when he becomes a little restless and begins moving around in your arms, it's time to put him down. If you pick up a guinea pig and squeeze too tightly or accidentally hurt him, he may squeal and give you a gentle nip on the hand.

Socializing with other guinea pigs

Guinea pigs socialize with one another and actually play, both young and old. They communicate with their bodies and with sounds. Nose rubbing is common, body rubbing and running in circles are favorite pastimes.   On occasion, they will sniff under one another's chin. With introduction of toys, they can play together. They will have periods of running after one another, hiding, squeaking and whistling, climbing all over one another and pouncing.

Normal behavior for guinea pigs can also include "head butting" where two pigs will stand opposite one another and "butt" noses/heads. This is dominance behavior and does not usually cause problems. Another dominance behavior is to chew on one another's hair.

Do guinea pigs play with toys?

Guinea pigs do play with toys. They enjoy investigating an empty box, perhaps with a hole in one side. An round oatmeal container is good, especially if it is open at both ends, and they will be happy with the empty cardboard tube from a roll of paper towel. A baby's sock with hay in it that can be lifted and thrown around is good. There is no need to buy expensive dog/hamster/cat squeaky toys, these tend to frighten the guinea pig rather than invite play. Bird/cat toys with bells, feathers, mirrors and wooden beads will also scare him.

Breeding and newborn guinea pigs

Female guinea pigs can be bred at five to six weeks of age, and males at about six to seven weeks of age. Because of this, you can sometimes have a young female -not yet fully grown herself- having a litter. Females should NOT be bred after they are a year old. They will have a litter of one to five pups, sometimes up to seven. They carry the babies for about six-seven weeks, and when the pups are born, they are born fully furred, have open eyes and come equipped with teeth.

In nature, guinea pigs are prey animals for large birds and land predators, and any baby born has to be able to sustain itself almost from the minute it is born. Mother will nurse the babies for a few days to a week. At about one week the pups will start chewing hay and eating solid food. The babies should be sexed as quickly as possible after they stop nursing and the sexes separated to avoid overpopulation and inbreeding.

Guinea pigs in large herds can pair male-female for life. If a female is not bred, she can go into heat every 2-3 weeks. Within a day or two of giving birth, she will go into heat again and a real possibility of "back breeding" can occur. This is potentially dangerous for the female and should be avoided.

How do you sex a guinea pig?

Pick up the guinea pig and gently turn him upside down, so he is belly up. Look at the genital area between the hind legs and notice a Y-shaped opening. Both sexes have the Y-shaped opening, but the female will have a small round area of skin in the lower end of the "V part" of the Y. The male will have a small penis head, it will look like a very small button, also located in the V part of the Y. With gentle rubbing/tapping on the area, the penis will harden and rise and in older males the testicles can be visible. In females, the entire area of the Y might swell and open a little.

Spaying/neutering a guinea pig is usually not an option. With surgery on that small an area on that small an animal, along with anesthesia, the entire procedure can be quite costly. It is easier just to separate the sexes and keep them separated to avoid unplanned litters.

How long does a guinea pig live?

The lifespan of a guinea pig in captivity is usually from five to seven years, although guinea pigs living up to eight or nine years is not uncommon. An elderly guinea pig will spend a lot of time in a corner of the cage resting. He will not be eating much, and gradually his coat will take on a "spiky" appearance. If there are other pigs around him, he will gradually seek more and more solitude and will turn to face the corner of the cage. If there is hay, he'll sometimes try to hide under the hay or spend most of his time in his "house."

Chapter Six: Diseases and Sickness in Your Guinea Pig

What about diseases in guinea pigs?

Guinea pigs are sturdy animals and by nature healthy, but disease can quickly kill them. Often they do not show symptoms of illness early on, so by the time you notice something being "wrong" with your pig, his disease can be pretty advanced. Pigs can have diabetes, urinary tract infections, glaucoma and arthritis. They can develop a respiratory infection with mucus from eyes and nose, and can have an abscessed tooth which makes it painful for him to chew/eat. A foot can become infected if the pig steps on a piece of hay, and the hay breaks the skin causing an abscess, which would make it painful for the pig to move around. A piece of hay can also pierce an eye and create an infection. Outside factors can also play a role such as mites or mange.

Diseases in guinea pigs:

- Respiratory infections
- Urinary tract infections
- Diabetes
- Glaucoma
- Blindness
- Arthritis
- Abscesses

- Arthritis
- Mange
- Mitcs
- Malocclusion
- Scurvy

How do I know if my guinea pig is sick?

If you notice that your guinea pig is not eating and is leaving behind food that he would otherwise have eaten, that is a sign he is not feeling well. Does he even want his favorite foods? If he has discharge or bleeding from the nose, eyes or any other place, he may have an infection or an injury. Is he drinking more or not drinking at all? Does he sit in a corner of the cage or hide in his "house"? Is he limping? Does he have a "sour" smell? All of these things are cause for concern and he should see a vet right away.

Can I take my guinea pig to a dog and cat veterinarian?

Most veterinarians can and will treat guinea pigs, however, a veterinarian who specializes in "pocket" animals and/or exotic animals is a veterinarian who knows guinea pig diseases, medication and medication dosages.

If your veterinarian prescribes antibiotics for your guinea pig, it is often in the form of drops. These drops can be added to water in the water bottle, but the water bottle will have to be cleaned vigorously every day. Some drops have an orange or apple flavor which will draw the guinea pig to drink.

Another option is to invest in a small syringe or eye dropper, put the drops into the syringe/dropper and squirt the drops into the back of the animal's throat. Wrap your fingers around the animal's mouth and nose and gently blow on his face. This will force the animal to swallow, and the medicine will go down easily.

If your guinea pig has a skin infection, usually the veterinarian will shave the affected area and apply a cream to the area. It is easiest to do this with your finger, touching gently the sore areas. Sometimes guinea pigs have a medication to take for mange that has the consistency of toothpaste.

The easiest way to give that medication is the same as with the drops: Measure the amount he has to have, open the mouth and put the medication as far back in the mouth as you can, close his mouth and gently blow him in the face. The medication is usually bitter and the pig will try to get the taste out of his mouth, so having a small piece of apple, parsley or corn will usually distract him. A pig with mange needs to be isolated from other pigs; most mange types are highly contagious. His dishes, water bottle, hay and shavings will also need to be kept apart from other pigs.

Chapter Seven: Guinea Pigs and Other Animals

Do guinea pigs get along with other animals?

Guinea pigs are social animals and enjoy the company of each other and of other animals. If he is carefully introduced to a friendly dog or cat, and doesn't trigger the larger animal's prey drive, they will get along fine. I have paired my guinea pigs with rabbits and some of my dogs and cats and have had success with that. However, introducing a guinea pig to a second guinea pig usually takes time as guinea pigs can get a little territorial about their cages, food and "house." If it is a guinea pig female being introduced to another female, usually within a day or two, they will bond and be fine.

An easy way to introduce two same-sex guinea pigs to one another is to do it right after cleaning the cage and putting the first pig back. If you bring a new pig into a cage that smells/has markings of the first pig, there will be territorial squabbling. If you bring the new animal into a cage that has no scent of the first pig and then quickly offer a distraction in the way of a treat, things will go a lot better with less squabbling.

Introducing an adult male to another male - even a young male- can be tricky and will require time, supervision and care. Sometimes the two males will accept one another, and sometimes they won't and will have to be separated. However, two litter mate mates who stay together usually form a close bond and will be fine unless there are females around. Sometimes just the smell of a female -especially a female in heat- will trigger a fight between two boars who were otherwise fine. However, as a rule, guinea pigs will get along with other herbivores, and seem especially fond of rabbits.

Guinea pig boars who fight can be severely injured; the fighting can escalate into full blown warfare where the two animals go for each other's lips, ears, face. It can be very bloody and can cause cracked/chipped teeth, ripped ears, lips and scratched eyes. Boars can also take out large chunks of each other's hair. A good way to separate two fighting males is to simply throw a towel over the two of them, pick them up and separate them. Don't put your hands down to separate them, your hand will be bitten instead. Check their injuries and make sure they are all right and offer them each a dark and quiet cage, preferably out of eyesight of one another.

A story about a companion guinea pig is found in author Gerald Durrell's story about using a guinea pig named Harvey to lure a gorilla out of a shipping crate. The gorilla had been shipped from Africa to Mr. Durrell's zoo in southern England, and had journeyed about a month when he arrived in England by boat. The crate with the gorilla was brought into the enclosure where he was to live with a flock of other gorillas, but a problem occurred when the gorilla refused to come out of the crate. This went on for about a week and Mr. Durrell in desperation finally introduced Harvey the guinea pig to the gorilla.

He put Harvey on the ground close to a tree about 10 feet away from the shipping crate in order took to try and lure the gorilla out of the crate. This was a great success except the gorilla climbed very quickly out of his shipping crate and took off for the top of the tree - about 40 feet high- taking Harvey the guinea pig with him. It took several days for the gorilla to come down, but when he did, he still had Harvey the guinea pig with him, and Harvey was just fine. Harvey lived out his days with the gorillas and spent many hours 40 feet off the ground in the tree tops, embraced and carried around by the entire gorilla family. They apparently slept with Harvey firmly in their arms and they were seen to groom him and feed him leaves and pieces of fruit.

Another story is about a young girl who had a pony and introduced her guinea pig to the pony. They became friends, and the guinea pig lived happily on the bottom of the pony's food trough where he had access to hay, grain, apples, carrots, corn and the occasional watermelon.

Chapter Eight: About using guinea pigs for research and guinea pig shows

Why are guinea pigs so popular for research?

Guinea pigs have several advantages for medical researchers: they are relatively large (compared to mice or even rats), and they are generally healthy, robust animals with a life span of about five to seven years. They are easy to care for and quite docile and don't put up much of a fuss being picked up, poked, probed, weighed and measured every day. Their internal anatomical configuration is much like human anatomy. They can produce several litters a year. For many years, the first developed new drug/treatment regimen has often been tried on guinea pigs, eventually graduating to "human guinea pigs" = the first to try something.

Where can I meet other guinea pig owners?

Most states have guinea pig clubs or Cavy associations with group meetings.

Are there competitions for guinea pig owners?

Many states have Cavy shows throughout the year. During the summer, there are 4-H shows where you can show your animal.

What is judged at a guinea pig show?

You can participate in county fairs and have your animals judged by a knowledgeable guinea pig judge. That judge will look at conformation (body build) of your animal, coloring, markings, breed and overall condition of the animal. It is important for the animal to be relaxed and calm so that when the judge goes to pick him up that he is not skittish and trying to hide. Sometimes, smaller shows are held outdoors in the summer months, and it is of the utmost importance that the guinea pigs have access to shade and clean water. If the show is not held indoors, a good thing to bring along is a cooler with frozen water bottles and a small fan, perhaps a table for the cage and a beach umbrella; that way the guinea pig can be in the shade and have a cool breeze blowing on him. The judge will sometimes ask you about your animal, and it is important that you know the name of his breed (Peruvian, Abyssinian, teddy-bear guinea pig, etc.). The judge will look at the animal's coat, and if he is a Peruvian, he will look at grooming. The judge will look at teeth, run his hand over the back of the animal and inspect ears, nose, feet and belly (to look for cleanliness). If the guinea pig is an Abyssinian, he will pay attention to placement of "whirls," looking for symmetry. The judge will sometimes also test the owner's knowledge and ask questions about the breed of the animal, etc.

More advanced guinea pig shows are held once or twice a year in most states and are usually sponsored by Cavy associations. There are magazines and websites to subscribe to that will notify you of upcoming events. At some of these shows you can see guinea pigs of all breeds, colors and sizes, and champions are then chosen for each breed, for each color in each breed, etc. Some owners have taught their animals to do tricks and will showcase that: one young girl had taught her three guinea pigs to climb a five-rung ladder, walk a tightrope and go down another five-rung ladder. Another taught her animals to follow in a straight line when she played a small whistle, six guinea pigs, one after the other making figure eights after her as she played the whistle.

Epilogue

A guinea pig can bring hours of joy to everyone, young and old. He will enrich your day-to-day life, provide hours of entertainment and give you something warm, gentle and furry to hold. He might not wag his tail when you come in the door, but he'll learn to associate you with food and socialization, and give a small squeak of delight when he sees/hears you come in the door. This is an animal with tremendous teaching power: He will teach anyone about responsibility, commitment, patience, observation and about being gentle. In return, he'll reward his person with endless hours of unconditional delight. Guinea pigs are very adaptable and can be had in an apartment as well as in a large house with a yard. They do not require much and give so much back.

About the Expert

      The author is a sixty six year old woman who has had and loved guinea pigs for more than sixty years. She and her family lived on the island of Puerto Rico, where guinea pigs are often kept in large pens outside the house and used as a meat source. The author's father had business dealings with a Puerto Rican gentleman and once at his house, noticed the pen with the guinea pigs. He asked the gentleman if he could have a small pup for his daughter -the author, who was then about four- and was given a box with six small guinea pig pups and that was the beginning of the author's love affair with guinea pigs. In the last 2-3 decades, she was known throughout Southern California as the Guinea Pig Lady. Veterinarians called and asked her to take in sick animals or animals they didn't have time for, and animals shelters had her on call. She also bred and raised guinea pigs for pet stores.

Recommended Resources

www.HowExpert.com

- Short "How To" Guides by Real Life Everyday Experts!

Made in the USA
Lexington, KY
19 December 2016